THEY DON'T KILL YOU BECAUSE THEY'RE HUNGRY, THEY KILL YOU BECAUSE THEY'RE FULL

THEY DON'T KILL YOU BECAUSE THEY'RE HUNGRY, THEY KILL YOU BECAUSE THEY'RE FULL

MARK BIBBINS

COPPER CANYON PRESS

PORT TOWNSEND, WASHINGTON

Copper Canyon Press is in residence at Fort Worden State Park in Port Townsend, Washington, under the auspices of Centrum. Centrum is a gathering place for artists and creative thinkers from around the world, students of all ages and backgrounds, and audiences seeking extraordinary cultural enrichment.

LIBRARY OF CONGRESS CATALOGING-IN-PUBLICATION DATA

Bibbins, Mark.

  [Poems. Selections]

  They don't kill you because they're hungry, they kill you because they're full /
by Mark Bibbins.

      pages cm

  ISBN 978-1-55659-458-8 (ALK. PAPER)

  I. Title.

  PS3602.I23T44 2014

  811'.6—dc23

                          2013025009

                    98765432 FIRST PRINTING

COPPER CANYON PRESS

Post Office Box 271

Port Townsend, Washington 98368

www.coppercanyonpress.org

Acknowledgments

Huge and heartfelt thanks to everyone—editors, interns, designers, proofreaders, et al—involved with the following concerns:

The Academy of American Poets, *Agriculture Reader*, Argos Books, All Along Press (Fort Gondo Poetry Series broadsides), Augury Books, *Bat City Review*, *The Book of Scented Things*, *Boston Review*, *Coldfront* (Poets off Poetry), *Conduit*, *ConnotationPress*, *Court Green*, *Dewclaw*, DIA Center (*Anthology of Silence*), *The Equalizer*, *Effing*, *Fence*, *Gulf Coast*, *The Journal*, *The Laurel Review*, *LIT*, *Maggy*, *New England Review*, *The New Yorker*, *Pax Americana*, *Poetry*, *A Public Space*, *Shampoo*, *Sink Review*, *The Sonnets: Translating and Rewriting Shakespeare*, *Starting Today: Poems for the First 100 Days*, *Telephone*, *THEthe Poetry*, and *Forklift, Ohio*.

Some poems in this book appeared in *The Anxiety of Coincidence*, an e-chapbook from *Floating Wolf Quarterly*; thank you to Christopher Louvet.

I'm grateful to the following people for prompts/assignments/invitations that led to poems: E.C. Belli, Melissa Broder, Sharmila Cohen, Iris Cushing, Timothy Donnelly, Jehanne Dubrow, Renée Gagnon, Arielle Greenberg, Dorothea Lasky, Paul Legault, Roddy Lumsden, Lindsay Lusby, Lynn Melnick, Steve Savage, Liz Clark Wessel, and Rachel Zucker.

Finally, love and gratitude to my friends and family, and to Copper Canyon for being like both.

Are you ready boys

Are you ready girls

Are you ready boys

Are you ready girls

—Throbbing Gristle

CONTENTS

THEY DON'T KILL
YOU BECAUSE
THEY'RE HUNGRY,
THEY KILL
YOU BECAUSE
THEY'RE FULL

Breakout Session

Before we say anything else I'd like
to point out that this coverage
is favorable to the user. I mean
I'm already a fan so I trust
the instructions, which seem
to tell us to reject a strutting self.
I'm able to choose that too.

*

Am I wrong or did the user leave
us lots of little choices. If we're
being led in wrong directions
in service of larger truths,
so be it: I will happily call a whole
school of red herrings my family.

*

Soon enough something pulls
me back to a photo of myself.
I don't remember who took it,
but it implies a phantom twin,
the kind of presence you reach
out to when you die.
Autobiography is still
the sincerest form of flattery.

*

There were things I couldn't say
before because I knew the group
would agree, one of which is that
I'm quite sure I've uncovered

the source of this terrible light,
not quite lethal, but the user
has given us a permission again,
and no matter how compelling
the light might be it has some
serious potential to degrade us.

*

In the end it's one of the user's
favorite solutions—water to water
to water to sex—but I don't mind
in the way I never do. He's drawn
a bath for everyone, and it's almost
as though I'm no longer afraid
there won't be enough room.

You'll Get Better Attention When You Die

We lived in a puddle before the wave.

If you remember either, the latter wasn't big enough.

We hurtle down the Grand Canyon
                with our pet chimp
                in a punctured raft:

Can you believe this is only 4000 years old!
                                        he exclaims
                                        or seems to,
                        hard to tell over the roar.

Give me better priorities
                or come insult me
                        if I make it to the riverbank
        so I won't want them as much.

Plants are lyric, animals epic,
depending on numbers of either—

        send my best to the underground
        fungus in the Northwest, the biggest
        one we've met.

The number of everyone I lost to AIDS in my 20s

        is small   compared to what.

                        Go on,

                wax beautiful

above what makes the world,

        glorious bastard years.

I Can Explain

We were upset

after the demons crashed our airplanes into us

We started hearing a lot about how they do things

in Afghanistan because that was one

of the places we were supposed to want to kill

because they had killed us

and one of the things they have there

is like a version of polo with a headless goat

instead of a ball

Polo is what

riding around on horses

and using long mallets to knock an object into a goal

on a playing field

And you said oh how awful savage people poor goat

dragging a headless goat carcass around

and then of course here we like football

!pigskin!

and you said oh how awful savage people poor pig

Unity, Utility, Ubiquity

if you're going to carry your gorgeous head around
in a sack
          let it be
this beige plastic one

wait, that's no good, it even says as much
on the bag
               right there
  next to the message
        about Jesus

what we learn from this is

        FAITH FIRST

        SAFETY SECOND

   the bag washed up on the beach
like some beautiful gift from an ocean that loves us back
       so I thought it fitting to recruit it

what a load of damage these gulls love
doing to loot we leave unattended
         as we work the water—

     good for them
and their sideways eyes, I say—let's run ads on bags
        for their avian religion
that calls it kosher
to disinter and circumcise
        Mormons with their beaks

     unless it's rude to bring up faith again

I'll close this beach and start a cornfield

       then I'm going to burn
              down that cornfield

and build a bank

     I can swim to save my own life at least

             then swim back
          to whatever's left of you

Evacuate the Premise

civilization on a string

sounds more sinister   than "the world"

stuttering is kisscousin   to an incantation

one we shouted when we came to
the creek and found it   full of math
but not so good for drinking

esteemed accomplice

much-lacked be-
loved   dearest

choice I didn't know I made

favorite first   and finally most

vulnerable spot

the trees release their latent fire at us

in photos of lightning

see
it eats upward
up

9

Pedagogy and Performance

Whatever the lesson was, it wasn't
taking. We awaited the information
in kind of a corporate way
and I kept wanting to go up
to the whiteboard and write
FEMININE MARVELOUS AND TOUGH
and ask, Is that what you're trying
to do.
      Sometimes it's hard to figure
out how to move. When cardinals
move, they're as imposing as cows.
They pull pornography
from abstraction.
      But let's also look
at us a few weeks ago: a scale
model of Seattle with its gleaming
library protruding like a jewel
from a navel—
      this was our best
self, not the contraption of drawers
and cranks that made our work;
not the surprisingly delicate bones
of Boba Fett, painted the same
colors as his armor; not the three
towheaded delinquents who
used the contraption in their
performance, then went home
after disparaging the audience
and showered together; not the cast
of my life filing into a wooden
amphitheater as my favorite band

started soundcheck in another
country.
     How would I get there
on time, even with half my friends
rooting for me, how do I get anything
done when as late as last night
someone started yelling CARDINAL
at the sight of blood soaking my sleeve.

In the Corner of a Room Where You Would Never Look

Warhol was right, he said athletes are fat

in the right places

and they're young

in the right places. Apparently

the next Godzilla movie has Godzilla

just running around eating everyone's

money and it's the scariest thing ever.

We can rub bug powder on the national

anthem and run that over the closing credits

as long as the singer manages to sing

I'm in love with everyone but you, almost

convincingly. A production team undoing

one another's pants

is How We Get Naked Now but tomorrow

morning all the cut-off parts of us are coming

back so get ready. Europe: you swear it exists

because you once had sex in it, and ideas.

Prepositions: that's where we all get sucked

under. Prepositions: the San Andreas

fault of meaning. Prepositions:

what came dislodged when our parents

hired operatives to kidnap us from cults

and deprogram us in the backs of vans.

Warhol was talking about the ass,

right, which we have come to understand

is the vessel of histories. That effect.

We put everything through

a translation engine

because we wanted to see the world.

Terminal

—tonight no one should be caught
fondling on stoops
    when they can climb up on
the fire escapes and screw—

    —what is all this fog
in the unedited air—

—I can't bite through
    it to you—

    —prudence is
        a no-headed fish
in a three-headed town—

—sickness draws a salary / a boarding pass
on human paper—

    —duress / duress / duress—

—horrors tucked into corners
of countries
    I can't give directions to—

    —the night my friend stopped cracking
jokes / we understood he would die—

—I had a vision of him being better than new
    and then he was gone—

    —decades hence I kick
    an inflatable globe
to him across the sidewalk—

—come up for some light

my hidden baby pigeon—

—cajole / cajole / kaboom—

Factory

He can say it was a painting
He can say we were the painting
Or that the painting wasn't painting
And we only happen to ourselves

We can say we kept things running
by creating distractions
from the hideous truth
of how things run

That we were broken
That we lingered near a broken factory
That we had broken

We can say that the disappointment
of slicing into a leek
and not finding the requisite layers
but a thick white inedible core
is not the disappointment
of approaching a sleeping animal
only to learn that it is dead
but it does nudge one slightly
further into despair

We said despair
We meant the strings of impossible
instruments that they made
in the factory
That we had seen
That were broken
That there were different paintings
That could be played as songs

We had seen other things
That we had seen
That had come unstrung
And blown between adjacent bridges
Whose river had presented us a city
That was broken
That we had been
That we were broken
That was our city
This was our city
that was a song replaying itself in the dark

Confidence

When a woman comes into the store,
points at me and says to her child,

Tell the man what you want, I turn around

to see where the man is.
Maybe I will visit him someday
in the Home for the Wildly Inarticulate,

for the Destroyed, for the Actual Man
Standing Where I Cannot Reach Him.

Don't expect I've seen the center
of anything, though I have been

privy to enough insane exchanges
to do with hygiene. Henceforth I ban you,

letter-shaped body parts, from
my purview: our last chat left
the taste of buckshot in my mouth.

It's early again, and late, when the birds

assume a tone neither mocking
nor judgmental, but something about

their exuberance is oppressive

enough to eat holes in the roof.
I just make the occasional collage
that falls apart when it rains,

wield my plaid umbrella like a sword,
and charge, exhausted, into the storm.

In Which the Pathetic Fallacy Wants to Even More

Frankly I don't follow this
strategy of yours wherein you
tell half the people on the island
you are a barista and the other
half that you are a barrister
  and they buy it.
                  Everyone else
believes and I continue to serve
as your wing-man as we snake
  among the aloe spikes.
                  You keep me so busy,
thwarting my every attempt
to find again a favorite stretch
of beach, when all I wanted
was to show you the pirate bar
  with the swings.
                  What else
has prevented me: relatives, railroad
tracks, paralysis, thickets of killed
umbrellas, cliffs impossible to scale,
a weeping jaguar, the fact
that it was 5:30, squishy brakes,
money, all my bent
  and voided sleep.
                  I wish I had
some idea but to admit I have
any at all is to risk that it is full
  of a sad nothing.
                  Huge lizards the color
of banged-up charcoal are shredding
one another beyond a cluster
of palms, their hisses curling the flat
green leaves and then disbanding

into the waves.
                That's a surfeit
of strategy right there but your faith
is still big enough to fit in a kayak
  that could be drifting in or away.

Desire Loves Disaster

I should have spoken clearly / made known

        the consequences of not accepting an offer

    even though I offered nothing
        and there were never any consequences

      trick question / minus question
      minus trick / minus minus

see how everyone heads for the shore

        to greet the unseen vessel
          that's devoured half the horizon

      but they find instead the moon's
      portrait sketched on the water

I say this / as though you were not everyone

        as though the moon had only a stump
        of chalk
      and nothing better to sketch

than its bleached and bloated self

            the beach is lined with lit-up skulls

          every eye a lighthouse / beaming into flotsam

            but they won't save us

my country runs to the edge
and throws itself in

when I said beach   I meant cliff

Spring, or, I Don't Know Everything Is Wrong with Me

Modes of transport deteriorate, scattering
into a list of insults, if a list can be said
to behave in such a way. One new find
I found en route: the etched initials of either

1.) the most famous poet
2.) depending on whom you ask
3.) as many beloveds
4.) an unlawful act of sexual congress.

This was to be the week I took up Reading
for Pleasure, the week to fracture something
ordinary if not quite expendable; but what
do we have here, a couple of low-slung stars.
              Someone's imagination comes now
and then to press down on me, even though
its source is surely nowhere doing the pressing.

The next adventure's my idea, he always
used to say, every other time.
Oh merde,

Monday's a holiday in America—
what a thrill to hear this from an American
mouth in any season, any town. Also pleased
to receive a friend's letter, which arrived
torn open and resealed with exactly
the kind of heavy-duty tape I would
expect him to own. I haven't been able
to read it for days,
                    but I've been admiring
a chunk of secondhand sun that tries
to illuminate the tape.
                  Wait. I'm going
to get a weapon and open it right now.

Honky

feels undermined by every morning he sleeps through.

Honky is straightening things out in Honduras.

Honky intercepts.

When Honky kicks it on K Street, cocks look up for miles around

and lengthen their lunch meetings.

Honky see, Honky do you hear what I hear.

The stem of time shoots through Honky's shoe and into the soil,

watered by the goatsmilk of regret.

Honky's gift theory: Gimme that.

When Honky finds a business partner to dick him over

near his allegory's end, he empties his meds into the commode.

Jeebus grant us ice hockey centerfolds and iron pyrite winking from the wall

of an abandoned mine in which Honky is slowly but exquisitely canarying.

When Honky drops a hankie, please to pick it up.

Honky made it past the menacing hurdle of his poor spelling.

The gravity of Honky's project makes a difference everywhere he rubs it.

A backhoe ran over Honky, uneasy to undo.

Honky must occupy himself with looking at this fucking honky.

Honky leaves on your abdomen a hickey the shape of Sicily

and plays several other instruments with parasitic enthusiasm.

Last year Honky trended toward the dark meat, eating the equivalent

of 87 five-legged chickens, but left a dozen three-egg omelets undisturbed.

If a sign says YIELD, trust Honky to gun it.

Huffy Honky, you can't keep repackaging a premise.

The Honky is painted on both sides.

As often as cosmology and Honky intersect, we have not yet determined

how to loosen the red shrinkwrap around our sibling sphere.

If spectacle breaks out, Honky is there, siren screaming, a volunteer fireman on fire.

Worst Things First

A bag of thank-you notes fell
on me and that was enough
art for one day. Culturally speaking,
it was more like a year
in the floral trenches, kicked off
with a single boneless kiss.
Poor sad demon in his poor dead tree—
or is it he who pities me, cockshy
quasihero with a latex lasso,
taking forever to measure

the dimensions of his confinement.
Certain other demons have smeared a flock
of sparrows on a blanket, the full filthy
price of a sky under which they smoked
their names. My prize is a set
of teeth, striptease at the nude beach,
audio files of decomposing stars
telling me, if they're telling me
anything, that theory's just another word
for nothing left to like.

Speedy

When burning guilt, add some more.
I'm hopped up on enough adrenaline
that whatever creature'd

eat me'd spit me right back out.
Fussy engine, turn the paddle
that sends the boat slopping up-

stream to a back-home-beaconing
town of sleepy assassins. What
makes an island: too few canoes.

Summer's Other

One long June, wrapped in its leather
weather holster, we were licked
to nearly death by dogs, then rose

from the same wet grave around
September, in which we would
accomplish nil,
the appendix-twitch molesting
my side. Wrong. The other side.

One last, one least surprising drink
taken to a garden, mixed with what
some samaritan squeezed out of clouds.

Thunderbride

My throat is full of sparklers
                                    making me a lighthouse
                    for a loveship   that can fly

Our mother monarchy
                    sweet land paternity

I'll eat their offspring's money   and let you have a bite

In wilder colors   I can love the copy of you
                    which is great   when we have breasts

He will breathe through contractions
          and she will heal the faceless
                    and use her eyes   to steel his legs

You must see that I'm eating for two sexes

Minimalism means   nothing making more
                    of what isn't there

     a green preconception
       divining a baby gender
               for which I qualified
     with braids ablaze   and stuck to my back

We are going to win   then make extra babies
       yes we make enough
          to make a country

Text unto the winged baby   the tiny pill of mystery
                    that makes me want to tickle the world
          until it starts barfing clouds

Make it free   is not the advice we paid for
          but a long song about the flavor of nowhere

                    and how we never fill it
        how I shave my buzzardy wings   to offend the sublime

While I'm quick to swallow   the heaviest business
                and quicker yet to modify that trash
        you have a poultice   for sudden holes

                        you have a knife in ten minutes
                you will marry a parent   and make it do
                        whatever you tell it

The raptor you were   does an end-run around sorrow
                        but I'm right here sweetness

                        out of the glass closet   voilà
                voilà   so what do you make of my baby

Tonight we bomb
Tonight we blitz
Tonight we barrage
Tonight we make the greater migration
Tonight our fabulous flock shits napalm on the criminal dads

For I am a figure   first of girls in orbit

                the best reason I have to eat your bed

I am spangled breasts   I am shaved
                like any birdboy   only huger
        than babies and ladybugs

                                one of either is precious
                        a million a menace

My inside is a live mine
                and I'm after the light that sustains the skin of women
                        scooping the spectacle
                where everyone freaks everyone

They will say how do you do Mister Ms. Thunderbride
and I will say I do it distorted

and you   will marry a million of you
in your twisted gown of flames

Medusa

RAINING

my enemies creep through the morgue
enemies croon in my doorway
[FIGS HANG FROM MORTAL TREES]
[IN THE GRAPHITE MONTH OF MAY]

SINGING

My enemies hide among corpses,
same distortion same fruition.

All of them, all of them
massive and becoming
more so. All thickening. I lay
the bodies in a field. There are
as many bodies in the palace
moat—they are their own
country, even if their shapes
are no longer theirs.

Deformity: what unmade me
has made its way here.

SINGING

Spoiled my master: resuscitation, amazing
remission; then bled myself when I
MURDERED THE MASTER, SPLIT HIM
INTO TWO MASTERS.

Now I do as they tell me, twice.

Built two sleds to drag him with
so the master can follow himself.

NB: There is a door to the village, through
which cherries and more cherries. These cherries'
only time. ONE BITE, one cherry, another;
so many they become monstrous and unmoored.

Hymn to servitude, nothing compels us
like nothing we knew.

Begged him to take my skin from me. Promised
to be good. Would show all my red useless work.

He poured answers from a cracked glass.
Left me to drown in the juice.

RAINING

in carbon May I woke in fever
in my muscles a murder of birds
[LEMONFIRE / GRIEF-COLLAGE]
in my burning crown of berries
in my darling martyrdom

in magnetite May to me come choirs of masters
[MY COVERLET / MY SACCHARINE COVE]
fly my suitors through espaliered fire

in iron May [MASK] a monstrous plum
in every mouth
in bronze May [FREAK] stunned and sliced
from my head [CHILDREN]

see they touch me
flies crowning our skulls

in pyrite May we hear only screams
of owls [SPARRING] and [LOWER] hyenas

branches of light stick to the lake
like burnt sugar [THE TREES ARE WEAPONS]
[TREES MUTELY SMEARING DISEASE]

alien hounds [STUNNED] in the woods
ripped apart even my allies [SHIELD]
wolves and martyrs mangle
a feminine history

climb into a decadence
wretch and pity in leaden May
[SLICE ME / SLICE MY / SLICE THEIR]
dying alien hours

SINGING

I am a stone morgue. You can hide
in here or among the grasses,
taller than horses on their way
to a farther country of fire.

Distended pools of purest poison [SWORDS]
through the August drone of locusts.
[UNSETTLED LUSTER. SQUEEZED-THROUGH
RIVERS. AND SKYDEBRIS AND DETRIMENT.]
SOUR DESIRE. Omens without accuracy. Suck
nightsplinters out of poked moons. Reckless
motions of animals as quinces fall
through treespace. Crushed like rotten piers.
Caught and churned in wolfpacks. Devotion.
Trauma. Caution. None can save them.
The peach sea engorged with men explodes.

– Master of violence, you plant one seed

– two sprouts uncurl.

– You may tend both [SLICK PORTAL, X'D-OFF

– MONEYFARM] but they're not yours.

– Mercifully.

– Mercilessly.

– Oily weeds.

– Stoke my envy, I will exile your mouth.

– Out of all the lakes in hell.

– They lap over the shores, open your tomb.

– Master, my tongue surge with money

– should [LOST] embers pour on us.

– No more perverted sermons.

– Numbness is my minister.

– Pain is your temple.

– My eyes [DEFECTION].

– Weapons, yes [INFLECTION] and sown

– from mutant seeds.

– Pluck my absence-fruits, eat of my solitude.

– So it's capital and secrecy.

– [STOLEN IN COPPERY MAY]

– May they crush you.

– May I catch them.

– Your death licks poison fruits into the past into

– now

– forever.

SINGING

I threw us through a bramble door
as proof: sentimental lyrics don't bust
a martyr's mettle anymore.

Murder a middle,
a terminal hell.

Hover at the entrance
of plausible mandarin limbo,
stunning in its breadth. Snow and steam.

My story earns me no money
so I told it in a fugue; passed months, mostly.
Poor lions wouldn't listen, so leopards
carried me in their mouths.

In a reservoir—   In uranium May—   Never—

SPLINTERING:

Cursed.

Dear Rotten Garden—

—who could bear to live next
to your wet humping sound—

—well I realize people do
absurd things in the world

they take off their skin
and don't touch me—

—from a height I am some sweet

girl   albeit one who squeezed
when she meant to swerve—

—having amassed a weddingful
of nuisances and sword-tasting—

—having moved prudently and shoeless

away   I could hear   you behind me

spitting perverted economies—

—also having been the painter
who takes your instructions

among them nothing
about painting

but what translates to *roll around on me*

like you're putting out a fire—

The Editors

We started experiments to do
with context. The way events
were perceived in context.
Also syntax. Benign interlopers.
To statements made in order
we introduced disorder. It even
felt like a rupture. Violent formal
gesture despite benign content.
Some of which had to do with beauty.
Some of which had to do with who
could twist beauty but no one could
recreate the sentences.
Each colorless device might have
been called pink or yellow or green
but the cards on which they were
typed are lost. Or fragments.
Whether or not a beauty
is benign. The point at which
game becomes ritual you've made
a more useful game but to whom.
You would call the fragment
a kind of violence but not
because of its importance
to the editors' choreography.
Here would be a decent place
to examine one of the cards
but no. As I said lost but what
if we woke not always
with the annoyance
of having glimpsed worlds
we've no tools to describe.
Who dislikes evidence
and how beautiful. What if one

of us were called Friend
and the other Friend of Friend.
What if we could explain
the marble cube at the center
of town and its function as a kind
of stage. Of literal chopping block
the editors used for others' phrases.
Who was the architect of reading
cards out of order. Monochrome
and no clue. His radical
idea and hers. We went looking
for radical once and found only
roots. We rendered each period
as a tiny heart and the relative
size of each heart allowed
us to measure our level
of attachment to each sentence.
Even to the font. To the root.
Still no content and it drove
some of us to despair. Others
to rhythm. To regroup
and to rename the cards. Yes yes
yes instead of each period a heart.

What Are Predators but Parasites That Kill You Faster

one conundrum is that you sew
a bunch of ghosts
together

only to end up with a smaller ghost

—you mend the hem / I'll tend the holes—

—chomp chomp choke / little bloodclot on the yolk—

thus you deviate as I scrape away
a cleaner spot

Short digression on decorating
the tree: find a woodchipper, feed
in honey, blankets, books. Treasure's
better decked in ketamine feathers
and wetforever lemons.

—hide us in a pit / rip the furtive flap / the stitched-up gut—

Short digression
on the middle of the desert:
we're in it.

under OTHER ACCOMPLISHMENTS

you can put "mimesis"
"snottiness"
"Ouija realness"

and "blinking when forbidden" please

love the desert
squeeze it
take it home
put it in a cage

with what's left of the ghost—

—even you should admit it's sweeter

than the pet leech
you used to keep

Burning Candygram

We call ourselves the future

country and mean to say final,
try to chew audibly enough

that we can find one another
in the unceasing night that swings

its black ax through us.

We're attuned to crash's register,
illnesses' inscriptions, sharks

lingering near the spigot that raises
and raises some more the seas.

I refuse to argue—no energy—

and I won't grovel. I need you
to enjoy me

nearly as much as an umlaut
changes the sound of the waves.

Almost as Good as What We Destroyed

Feigned outrage, real idiocy—how do we delete
what's onscreen when someone put a foot
through it last night. The perks

of taxis emerge as the bus goes over a canal,
then a cliff; if it helps to grip my hand
as we plummet, you can.

A book with no table of contents, no index—
you want to trust that waiting will
reward you with less waiting,

but I wouldn't. Any vehicle is terrifying when
it goes too fast on unfamiliar roads, and by
terrifying I mean beautiful,

a fluke of white and blue light. I want to address
a Vespa in the second person, want it to
respond, but it's done with me.

Not to be ignored, I invent an incline so steep
that when a truck ascends, it flips
over backwards—the same

sensation rips me out of sleep—in other
words, far too beautiful to bear.
A passenger recurs, always

in a different seat, and won't adhere
to my schedule, but I am too
weak to ask whether

we're running ahead or behind. Who would
know. When I melt this way I relish
the cool air forcing

me back inside my skin. Look around, there
are fewer possibilities, so let's call
what we do pedestrian, scrub

every other description. We've taken wing.
I offered you my hand before—
maybe you should take it.

The Bell Is a Recording

the skins of trains   are grimy and terrible

full of associations

                 I know this as someone
           who sits under a tree

       considering which end of his flashlight
        might dig out of the dark

           more terrible things

     paintings of this scene
        hang in museums

let them hang

let them hang

         let me find the medicine
        I brought here with me

             too much   and death

             too little   and same

    as if to suffer

            were an easier decision
              to have made

a music the dead effortlessly compose

which notes they use most   which rests

drag queens are superheroes

but there is no superhero
                with only the superpower
                of observation

because that would make
                        an insufferable superhero

                        constantly pointing

I'm doing noon

a project everyone can tell
                        when it's not done right   like cassoulet

a looped recording of an actor advises us
                to keep an eye on our stuff

                and not to fall on the tracks

the same message scrolls endlessly overhead

                        in orange pixels
                        and it must be working

I haven't fallen on the tracks yet

sorry to have made you

    say SUN
    out of the corner of your mouth

    MOON
    into your glove

    YES
    into the narrow trench

        further narrowing into never

Strategy

Be expert

or be no expert

citizen

Say nice things

make nice things

then let them *have* it

Prisons are for money and rape

You can see them from the highway

so you have some idea

Late night talk show joke

don't drop the soap

Ha ha funny rape

Nope

Pat Robertson Transubstantiation Engine No. 1

First I was fellating an African despot
for his diamonds, next I was paying

a hooker to give me back
my teeth. You think I'm kidding

about the diamonds, I was looking
also for some gold. I almost

sound cute,
right, like a steamed wiener

squished into a top-slit Wonder bun.
I unload a mouthful

of warm root beer
down the back of your neck

and tell you it's Jesus weeping
sweet brown tears of shame. Aim

your gutter
this way and give some back to me.

Pat Robertson Transubstantiation Engine No. 2

Well it turns out I'm totally activated
by donations. All you have

to say is the magic word,
ISRAEL, and everyone goes crazy.

If we didn't abuse the Bible
it would cease to exist. O heavenly

flogger you should be watching me
on cable right now.

These clouds
are looking like trouble, in these clouds

I'm looking for trouble.
See there, in the clouds, boiling

like a syphilitic
oatmeal snowman, that's my face.

Pat Robertson Transubstantiation Engine No. 3

We will serve you if you will get us free
from the French. Then we'll rest

a moment and bask
in all I've taken.

I asked: you gave: I snatched
candy from the collection plate and replaced

it with a baby.
My shtick's like a turkey

stuffed full of kleenex, my feelings
fuzzy as the mold

on the host my licks turn green.
Oh, how the Lord's light is good

as a fondle
when I catch it for you

in my gums.
Sometimes the little lady and I prefer

to call my pecker The Wishbone.
I don't know who's luckier

but all my wishes
work for me.

Pat Robertson Transubstantiation Engine No. 4

Jimmy in jail and I don't care,
Tammy crack up

and I don't care. Wait a sec, is it
the desert in here

or is my greased-up heart
all a-sputter like a skillet

at a Friday fishfry. Jesus sure
would appreciate

how I redeem things
using like or as,

even if my cue
cards are crooked. Half the fun

of end times
is always feeling full.

Pat Robertson Transubstantiation Engine No. 5

I don't have to be nice
to the spirit of the Antichrist

but oh the sweet caul fat of Falwell
melting on my tongue's

like a heavenly lozenge
in a blizzard of ash.

Jerry, that's my feeling. It tastes like loot
in a wallet he sat on

all day, rich
as a tobacco field in heaven.

Jerry, that's my feeling. We'll pray
for some miners and their parent

companies, which is where the real
action is, if you know

what I mean. *Jerry,*
that's my feeling. Jesus was all for share-

holder value, maximum
returns, and when he comes back

I'll chain him to a machine that turns
water into oil.

Pat Robertson Transubstantiation Engine No. 6

Mac and cheese for Christmas dinner,
Is that a black thing? Gosh,

the planet's weirder
every day I'm on it.

One day Jesus will hit us
like a ton of marijuana biscuits

but some of us won't be around
to see it. I mean, *why did you*

build houses where
tornadoes were apt to happen?

Sometimes I feel like
a stopped clock, except

one of us
is right twice a day.

I'll say it again with my mouth
full: *I think we've just seen*

the antechamber to terror.
Open wide.

~~Historical~~ Action Figures

Buzz Aldrin wants to colonize Mars—
well, not by himself, but maybe he can
be a consultant, which as far as I can tell,
is about the best job there is, better
than even astronaut or wildcatter.
Let's go to Mars. It's a great idea
because it increases the odds
of finding things on Mars
to kill. Cut a hole in Mars and what
comes out. Buzz Aldrin is an ~~historical~~
action figure at this point, but that's not
his fault, per se—he sounds like
a quarterback in a game of what
we care about instead of what happens,
while Haliburton sounds like a posh couch
or a horse with thicker-than-average legs
who wins all the races but is revealed
to be a robot. He gets to keep
the prize money anyway.
You fish, you wish you were robots
so you could drink the crude
that robots drink. You pelicans
you turtles you shrimp you know
the drill: IT IS WE WHO ARE IMPORTANT
when we swim down to the holes
we've punched in the world
and suck the money out.

The Perspective Fairy

Henry Fonda didn't die on you,
he just died. Carol Burnett

says this to Liz Taylor in
a movie so Liz gets wasted

and puts a shopping bag
over her head, or Carol

says it to make Liz
feel better after trying

and failing to kill herself with
a bag. Certainly we all need

a visit from the Perspective
Fairy now and then but you

have to be careful because
not just anyone

can play him.
Ernest Hemingway was summoned

to coax a friend down from a roof
with a cold-cream jar of opium

that Ezra Pound had left for him
with the instruction to bust it

out in case of an emergency—
really if these were the guys

in charge of my safety
I'd take to the roof too—

but when the friend finally
came down, he threw the jar

at Hemingway's head because he
knew that the real Perspective Fairy's

got gigantic wings you can
almost see through.

Bowerbird

I recently rescued a supermarket
bag from the crotch of a tree,

found fewer shields than souvenirs,
figured out how to game the pain scale

and opted not to. Water the color
of watery tea comes through

the light fixture on a holiday
when nobody can come plug it up

and make us regret complaining.
Nothing like a movie to remind you

that you never travel and a lot
of almost fornicating happens

a mere floor or two above the one
you're on. Shoulder, TV flicker, flash

of back. I'll make up a name and try
to affix it to whoever left these four

white doors on the sidewalk, which
I dragged home two and one

at a time. In daylight they reveal
the smudges left as tenants groped

one spot, then the next—hall, stairwell,
street, the mess just beyond, forest

on the opposite side of the globe.
There's always the absurd

woven into each nest I build and hop
around, waiting for the right one

to wander in. The right one
is the one who wanders in.

The Year Is Always Two Years Ago

When the barber puts the smock on me
I become a secret with a head. But even
this is about to change.

*

I was mute most of the season we met,
and couldn't tell you how I'd spent
nearly twenty lucky previous years,
wherein cars about to run me down
made sudden and dramatic turns
onto side streets or on-ramps,
leaving me stunned but not quite killed.

*

During that time, songs came
and secretly never went, drifting
brightly over beaches, fields, and towns.

*

You gave me a medium neither air nor water
on which to survive. Has anyone ever taken
a photo of an angel smirking—I bet I could
get one to do it, if not to hold still.

*

Being on TV has never been so easy
says a lunatic voice on the radio. If I'm dead
when you find this, it will be sad or funny

or both, given our sagging empire,
or neither if you never knew me.

*

Those couples slumped against themselves,
sleeping on trains, they must be that tired.

Junior National Treasure Cemetery

in case you are promiscuous / or merely forgetful

    I've carved your name on half the trees

of this burnt forest / to help you find home

whether you arrived umbilical / or toothing through an egg

    exploit your former form / for the larger culture

    everywhere I smell scorched

meat I would not have eaten / even if cooked perfectly

    the stench grabs my throat and shakes

bodies walk out of hospitals / emptying the nurses' tip jars as they go

unless you're Edward Gorey / don't tell us too early

    that there's arsenic in the pudding

    we're willing to pay extra / for a little more suspense

Grief!

Once I told someone
he should call his poem that
but I don't know how
it turned out.
You could say Good
magazine or There's a celebrity
on the fire escape
behind you,
and enough people
would still want to hear
the part about fire. I have
one enemy
but we don't know it yet.
When we do we will meet up
at the balloon show
with a box of pins.

Better Than Okay, with Androgyny

As long as you're not William F. Buckley,
whose disdain would sustain me now,
I will apologize when the air stops moving.
The newly saved pole-dance a million
sour excuses. Ambidextrous
fetish-finders pull their bows
across a century and call it music,
but who breaks my harp, what David
swings my stones.
                An orchard is burning
but you avoided how such transactions
fuck with time. I don't have anything
much—what useless fire is light,
what distant mobile mouthing.
Most excellent pre-op calls me Baby
in the bar when I offer her some ice
because I don't have anything else.

Being Our Pictures

the children propagate, perpetuate / lo, I am one of them

they do not recognize their duplicity / lo, I am complicit around them

nothing I say undoes me, alas / between you, end me

what makes no children

should you come back don't hock / the real jewel of indignation

how can I add value / if I can't call meetings

on flirting: to be bad at it / makes you good at it

on syntax: my meme / do me no favors

on novels: lo, disappointy / on the rogue antecedent:

don't play along / but die if we do / and die if we do

A Place I Plan to Admire as Much as One I Can't See

Every day I go to your building
and deliver the same news,

even though it changes
every other hour. So red where

you live and no one moves
inside, though the bricks

reveal implications of light.
A husband said *I want exactly*

what you want but not
exactly to me—you can't

make those decisions for them
and not my story anyway:

HI I NEGLECT YOU BYE.
What about a paragraph

behaves most like a room
was another thing we didn't spend

a lot of time
worrying about, but time you can

usually squeeze as you might
a little gray paint

from a tube—only spelled
G-R-E-Y or named

something else altogether,
like an emotion made of clay

or an animal they claimed
to have invented

for the occasion, but was
actually ennui and so

not very emotional after all.
Just another excuse, I like

those too. Our town
was built near if not quite

under water
and when we weren't trying

so hard to vanish
into it we rode, three

to a whale, abandoning
unmade beds behind us.

A lot of soldiers were more
handsome than would have been

tactful to note, and on a secret
dolphin assignment. A former

beau boated by, dragging behind
him the net of his new demeanor

—to be spared's not too much
to ask for till it is—but I can't

get used to the flying fish staring
me down, and how can anything

possibly add up when we hear
a dog barking this far out at sea.

The Anxiety of Coincidence

Your object will have made a good subject
and I should get to tell you so—the bird
with a beak but no mouth, we hear him only

when it's night in the Dominican Republic
and Syria at the same time. They will find
your marginalia useful in this ink, so try

to spare some. I took dictation only from you,
for whom verbs were nothing and tense
everything. See the difference, they kept asking,

but it wasn't a question. See how enormous:
camel hauling an empty wheelchair, conspiracy
of hangman men, dried-out song that makes

it snow. You realize we could have walked
home in the hours taking inventory took, jack
of no traits. Bird with no wings.

My Brightness Button

On the airplane I own I need you
to behave, and not like a moth
happening upon its first caterpillar—

really, what an important moment.

Knowing the cartoon of my airplane
is creeping imperceptibly across maps
on tiny screens on the backs
of the passengers' seats makes

me feel pretty famous, famous

as a rare but relevant moth. I wish
I knew all the money I have

by heart. I like to hear my voice
on the speakers, reminding everyone
that I am owner of this immaculate
silver monster and that we are so

much higher than the orange

lights of the cities spreading like
crushed spiders across the globe.

There's an avenue down there
in Irondequoit that I want someone
to write a musical about so we can

all parachute down to Irondequoit

and see it together. The flight
attendants have completed
their essays and they're pretty
good. In fact they're perfect

but I'm correcting them anyway;
I like to delete and close things up.

Look Who Came Dressed as the Sun

What's worse, energy or ambition?
We used to say sincerity, now we can't—
the wind not so easy to utter either
when it's filling up your mouth.
Figure out something edible, a seed
at the source but nothing occurs.
If you write "ironic detachment"
in your orange notebook again
I'm going to throw it into a fire
even if I have to make a fire.
When one gets a handle on blame—
it's beneficial for the critic to have
a few extra fingers—it allows one

to fabricate more useful than usual
perversions. A man stepped off the train
holding a pale green thing which might
have been a takeout salad or maybe
a lizard filling the cradle of meat
his fingers made. I tried to see
but he was gone—that's how a lot
of stories end when someone smarter
than you doesn't like you either.
It's basically always me in here
but I'm less crucial than the light
that shoots through every window
I walk by and floods me almost with joy.

Poem That Wants to Know If We Need Anything from the Store

Delores Grocery, pray stop
boasting about your

connections or enough
of your clients will begin

demanding a discount far deeper
than you can muster. Your brand

of whimsy
is unsexy, you don't see

go-go dancers acting all whimsical
and what about their dinero

is the wrong
color. Delores Grocery, please, I'm really

asking you. Delores Grocery,
I'm starting to worry

about your relationship
to capital—maybe only

because I've been reading Chris Nealon,
but possibly you've been, too.

Delores Grocery, make me
mind my business

and forgive me, I've never
even set foot in you.

Poem That Wants to Know When You're Taking out the Trash

Most of the people from the present
are gone now; we never held them
very tightly, but what our wounds lack

in depth, they make up for in breadth.
If living is a sort of punishment or reward,
well there's no way I can finish

that sentence. I'm so young, I have
to show you how many years
with my fingers. The only thing worse

than advice is an opinion. This paper
bag is full of them, and a lone
hydraulic squeal is telling me

it's garbage night. The moon agrees,
which you may think it automatically does,
but more and more it seems it won't.

Poem That Wants to Serve You Comfort and Despair

On the horizon we saw it: a spot
of racism. A little black boat full
of bitches, with BITCHES LOVE SONNETS
embroidered on the sail. Its haul
festered and boiled in our belly;
see, it wasn't just the bad clams,
but a spectacular case of the clap.

This new system makes it easier
to track and to hasten our demise,
the future devoured from beneath us,
like the pitchblack timber of the bitch
boat, by cartoon termites who merrily
assert that it's much harder to untie
a wet knot than a burning one.

Poem That Wants to Be Something Rather Worse

A dead CEO admonishes me
to do what I love, which he can't
see me doing. I only need

a clean place to lie
around, to see a few decent things.

*

I'd feel fortunate to have half
of that, but which half.

*

Also I look up to see everything
has gone a shade of purple that should
only last a few minutes but goes on
for an hour because of the clouds.

And why is that, an equinox
or its afterbirth staining everything
some other words for purple.

*

He says:
Go find them all for me
and keep maybe one for yourself.

Give them to me and invent more
and I will acquire them.
Hand over the ones
you were in the middle of

making and I will
tell the world I made them.
They are mine—Lilac™ | Violet™—

and I will kill you to impress
upon you that I can.

Poem That Wants to Use Revelation 3:16 as an Epigraph

A guy who was a regular
at the bar where I used to work

we called Peckerhead because
he looked sort of like a balder

Ginsberg, who looks like a pecker.
Well I have no idea how Ginsberg looks

now, but it's probably pretty
peckeresque. Peckerhead drank dollar

drafts and was no doubt ten times
smarter than all us smartass bitchy

barmaids put together, maybe he
was a botanist or an actuary

or had some other clever gig. I felt kind
of guilty about it, even though we never

called him Peckerhead to his face, as far
as I know. Ginsberg died April 5 (1997),

birthday of Colin Powell (1937), so happy
b-day C.P. and happy d-day A.G. Inevitably

we would get loaded during our shifts, before
we killed ourselves or caught you-know-what

or left town before either of those things
or worse happened. Did I read somewhere

that Ginsberg fucked a guy who fucked
Whitman? Fucked/got fucked by? So stinky,

who cares. I must not see what fucking
is, other than stinky. If I had anything

to say about gender I'd already
be fucking you or paying Peckerhead

to fuck you. I think he was gay too.
All the girls we saw after work

at the porn store, their skin was
the color of a three-month-old

plaster cast. If I could make you
a real simile it would be like when

I turn into a boy I will wag
a pecker at you like a dirty mop

until it cracks and flops around like
my broken leg. No girls better

go there, Peckerhead always said,
no girls in the porn store.

Poem That Wants to Be Less Amazed by a Man in a T-Shirt That Says

BITCHES AIN'T SHIT
BUT HOS AND TRICKS

Oh—it's from a song? Sorry

to have missed the memo
on acceptable sexist invective:

bitches, you know the words,
so why not sing along.

One of my ex's relatives
said about another relative

She should only get cancer

and whoever John Lennon was
paraphrasing said poetry is what happens

when you're making other poems.

One way for me to care about something
is to stack it next to what I forgot,

and maybe you'd care too,
if I weren't so busy

trying to explain,
if I weren't so easily amazed.

Similes Liberation Army

It's like Miss Moore breaking into
Whitman's place on Ryerson Street,
eating his stuffed parrot, then keying

every car on the block. Chronology,
though not a verb, is a crap thing to do,
even to things we dislike.
All hat,

no hat.
Like declaiming the dictionary,
like setting the Betty Crocker oeuvre
to music, like painting paintings

of half the numbers until nothing else
is like. Don't kill your idols, just
compare them. That will kill them.

The Beginning of How We Started Dying

I was praying to Santa, who has never
recognized my birthday, which could
explain why this year I received a copy
of the Oblivion Social Register
and a used pop-up turkey timer, both
of which I now use as ballast as I bob
in a giant pot, cannibal-dinner style.
As it says on my tombstone,
LAZY BUT FUNNY.
                    Add me to the list
of almost notable homos who passed
on the South Pole—I elsewise go
where I am called upon to edit
down the news. I'll have to order
a bigger box for all my drugs,
but hurry, the last boat leaves
on the hour.
                    I've started praying
for something excellent next year,
which I'll never get if I say what it is.

Further Strategies for Trapping the Dead

A perilous poetics balanced in a doorway

      feet up   its shadow

      thus an ad hoc tarot poetics

An acquisitive poetics in a range

      of verdant tones implying undulating snakes

A mouthy poetics

A poetics of idols on an altar

A poetics of winnowing demented candidates

A poetics of quarters of sedatives

      and halves

Another poetics of a different doorway

      past which the clientele is filing

A poetics of oh no   what are these   *symbols*

      or chickens hastily butchered

A celebrity poetics and a poetics

      of plain old longing

A vulture poetics

First one then of all of these hunkered in a series of rooms

      thus a poetics of variable thresholds again

An oxymoronic poetics

A discursive poetics

A flaccid poetics

A peachy poetics

And one of pronouncing it like "politics" and noting

       any change this makes to the room

A placid objective poetics of everything

       online   last   year

A poetics of uncles and a Johnny-come-latently or two

Ever and always   one of upgrades

A predatory poetics

The poetics of a monochrome palate

       but within it

       jostling shades

The poetics of the theremin

       which like language you play

       without touching

Witness

I.

Religion happens after birds eat
berries and carry the seeds overseas
in their bellies, language gets
around on the condition that bees
drag it out of flowers. Punk and dub
had to travel in other vessels,
the latter made of space
and the former none or at least
too little. Songs are always built
and dismantled at the same time,
always demanding to see
pictures of themselves.

New York London Paris Munich
Munich Paris London New York
Paris Munich Paris Munich
London London New York New York

A few people are still alive, you'd
have heard them if they'd sung,
a few others too, if they'd
a sound among them to sing.
The eyes!
If history ever comes for them,
the eyes can hide in the mouth.

2.

abjectness abruptness absoluteness abstractness abstruseness accurateness acquisitiveness acuteness adroitness aggressiveness aimlessness airworthiness alertness allusiveness aloneness aloofness amateurishness animateness apprehensiveness appropriateness aptness arbitrariness archaicness arduousness artfulness articulateness artificialness assertiveness astuteness attentiveness attractiveness audaciousness augustness awareness awfulness awkwardness backwardness badness bagginess baldness balkiness bareness baroness baroqueness barrenness baseness bashfulness bitterness blackness blamelessness blandness blankness blasphemousness bleakness blessedness blindness bloatedness blueness bluntness boldness boorishness bounciness boundlessness boyishness brashness braveness brazenness briefness brightness briskness brittleness broadness brokenness brotherliness brownness bumptiousness burntness burstiness business callousness calmness candidness capaciousness capriciousness carefulness carelessness casualness cautiousness cavalierness ceaselessness ceremonialness charitableness chasteness cheapness cheerfulness cheeriness cheerlessness childishness chilliness chivalrousness chubbiness cleanliness cleanness clearness cleverness closeness cloudiness clumsiness coarseness cockiness cohesiveness coldness combativeness comeliness commercialness commonness compactness competitiveness completeness conciseness concreteness conduciveness connectedness consciousness contagiousness contemporariness contrariness coolness copiousness correctness covetousness coziness craftiness craziness creativeness credulousness creepiness crispness crudeness currentness curtness cuteness cutesiness daintiness dampness dangerousness darkness deaconess deadliness deadness deafness dearness deceitfulness decisiveness defensiveness definiteness deliberateness denseness destructiveness devoutness dimness dinginess directness dirtiness discreteness disingenuousness disinterestedness disjointness distinctiveness distinctness divisiveness dizziness doggedness drawnness dreariness drowsiness drunkenness dubiousness dullness dumbness duskiness dutifulness eagerness earliness earnestness earthliness easiness edginess effectiveness effortlessness elaborateness electricalness elusiveness emptiness endlessness enormousness enviousness erroneousness evenhandedness evenness exactness excessiveness excitedness exclusiveness expertness explicitness expressiveness exquisiteness extraneousness extraordinariness eye███████ faintness fairness faithfulness faithlessness falseness familiarness fanciness fastness fatness fearlessness feebleness ferociousness fewness fickleness fierceness filthiness fineness finiteness firmness fitness fixedness flatness fleetness flimsiness floridness floweriness fondness foolishness forcefulness foreverness forgetfulness forgiveness forthrightness forwardness foulness frankness freeness freshness fretfulness friendliness frightfulness fruitfulness fullness funniness furtiveness fuzziness gameness gaudiness gauntness gayness generousness gentleness genuineness ghastliness giddiness gingerliness gladness glassiness goldenness goodness governess gracefulness graciousness grandness gratefulness gratuitousness graveness grayness greatness greediness greenness grimness grossness grubbiness guiltiness habitualness hairiness handedness handiness handsomeness haphazardness haplessness happiness hardheadedness hardheartedness hardiness hardness harebrainedness harmfulness harmlessness harmoniousness harness harshness hastiness hatefulness haughtiness haziness headstrongness healthfulness healthiness heartbrokenness heartiness heartsickness heaviness heedlessness helpfulness helplessness heterogeneousness hideousness highness hoariness hoarseness holiness hollowness homelessness homesickness homogeneousness honorableness hopefulness hopelessness horribleness hotheadedness hotness hugeness humaneness humanness humbleness humorousness huskiness iciness idleness illness illustriousness imperviousness implicitness impressiveness inadequateness inappropriateness inclusiveness incompleteness inconsiderateness incorrectness indebtedness indecisiveness indefiniteness indigenousness industriousness ineffectiveness inertness infiniteness ingeniousness innocuousness inquisitiveness insidiousness instantaneousness intentness intrusiveness inventiveness inwardness irateness jauntiness jealousness jerkiness joblessness joyousness justness keenness kindness lameness languidness largeness lateness lawlessness laziness leanness levelness lewdness lifelessness lightness likeliness likeness limpness lioness literalness littleness liveliness liveness Loch Ness loftiness loneliness looseness loudness lousiness loveliness lowness ludicrousness lusciousness lustiness madness maleness maliciousness manageableness marvelousness meagerness meaningfulness meaninglessness meanness meekness mellowness melodiousness memorableness mercenariness meritoriousness messiness methodicalness mightiness mildness milkiness mindfulness minuteness miscellaneousness mischievousness miserableness mistiness moderateness modernness moistness momentariness momentousness monotonousness moodiness morbidness motionlessness mournfulness muddiness mustiness mutableness muteness mysteriousness naiveness nakedness narrowness nastiness naturalness naughtiness nearness neatness needlessness nervousness newness niceness niggardliness nimbleness nobleness noisiness nonbusiness nosiness nothingness numbness obliqueness obliviousness obviousness oddness odiousness odorousness offensiveness officiousness oldness ominousness oneness opaqueness openness oppositeness orderliness ordinariness outspokenness paleness passiveness pastness patroness peacefulness perfectness permissiveness persuasiveness pervasiveness pettiness physicalness picturesqueness pinkness pithiness plainness plaintiveness playfulness pleasantness plumpness poisonousness politeness pompousness poorness populousness positiveness possessiveness powerfulness powerlessness precariousness preciousness precipitateness preciseness preparedness presentness presumptuousness pretentiousness prettiness primeness primitiveness promptness proneness properness protectiveness punctiliousness quaintness qualifiedness qualmishness quarrelsomeness queasiness queerness questionableness quickness quietness quirkiness raciness raggedness rancorousness randomness rankness rareness rashness rawness readiness realness reasonableness rebelliousness recentness receptiveness recklessness reddishness redness reflexiveness relativeness relentlessness reliableness religiousness remarkableness remoteness repetitiveness repleteness representativeness resistiveness resoluteness resourcefulness respectfulness responsibleness responsiveness restfulness restiveness restlessness restrictiveness retentiveness richness ridiculousness righteousness rightfulness rightness ripeness riskiness roadworthiness robustness roominess rosiness rottenness roughness roundedness roundness rowdiness ruddiness rudeness ruggedness ruthlessness sacredness sadness safeness saltiness sameness savageness scantiness scarceness secretiveness selfishness selflessness senselessness sensitiveness separateness seriousness sexiness shadiness shakiness shallowness shapelessness sharpness sheepishness shiftiness shininess shortness shortsightedness shrewdness shrillness shyness sickness silliness simpleness sinfulness singleness skillfulness slackness sleepiness sleeplessness slightness slipperiness sloppiness slovenliness slowness sluggishness slyness smallness smartness smoothness smugness sneakiness snugness soberness softness solemnness solidness solitariness sordidness soreness soundness sourness spareness sparseness speechlessness spiciness spiritedness spitefulness springiness squareness starkness statuesqueness statutoriness steadfastness steadiness steepness sternness stickiness stiffness stillness stinginess storminess stoutness straightforwardness straightness strangeness strictness stringiness stubbornness sturdiness stylishness subtleness succinctness suddenness suggestiveness suitableness sulkiness sullenness suppleness sureness surfaceness surliness sweetness swiftness talkativeness tallness tameness tardiness tartness tastefulness tastiness tautness tediousness temperateness tenderness tenseness thankfulness thanklessness thickness thoroughness thoughtfulness thoughtlessness tidiness tightness timelessness timeliness timidness tininess tinniness tiredness tirelessness tiresomeness togetherness touchiness toughness transitiveness treacherousness trickiness trimness trustfulness trustworthiness truthfulness typicalness ugliness unaccountableness unadaptableness unadaptedness unaffectedness unawareness uncleanness unconformableness unconsciousness uneasiness unevenness unfairness unfaithfulness unfitness unfriendliness ungratefulness unhappiness uniqueness unkindness unlikeness unnaturalness unpleasantness unreasonableness unselfishness unsteadiness untidiness untruthfulness unwieldiness unwillingness unworthiness uprightness usefulness uselessness vagueness validness variableness vastness verticalness viciousness vileness villainousness vindictiveness vividness wantonness wariness wastefulness watchfulness weakness weariness weatherproofness weightlessness weirdness wellness wetness whiteness wholeness wholesomeness wickedness wilderness wildness wiliness willingness wimpiness wiriness wistfulness ███████ wonderfulness woodenness wordiness worldliness worthiness worthlessness worthwhileness wretchedness wryness yellowness youthfulness zealousness

By the Number 3

Can we back up and read
that sign again, the one

trying to tell us about a band
playing on a beach lined

with pine trees, very old.
If the internet doesn't work

there you have to build
your own. Let's rewrite

the constellations
so they read as all kinds

of fruits: here we see
the Grape Cluster reclining

just above the indigo treetops;
Can of Lychees keeps tampering

with my weekly horoscope
but I don't know how.

Thus magic shuffles reluctantly
toward us and if you claim

you can organize it you should
be making a joke. Look

at a 3 the wrong way
and all you see is your own

wretchedness. If you look at 3
in a different way you might

see a fortunate mouth getting
ready to kiss. You used to

feel like you were always
going to the same place

but it didn't hurt and other
times the ocean glowed

so blue it broke
half your bones.

Our Fairy Decorator

My parents went to Paris
and all I got was theory.
I believe in parthenogenesis,

in embracing the limitations
of direct address in theater.

I believe ever less
of what is spewed at me.

On the side of a new building
someone spray-painted
WHATEVER HAPPENED TO ANARCHY?

I reckon the question answers
itself, but just to make sure,

I'm going to take some red
nail polish, paint quotes
around WHATEVER and erase

the question mark.

I believe in the pillow-tossing gene,
mapped out somewhere

on an unfathomable expanse
of traits—thanks for the insights, fruit flies,

but we no longer require your services.

I believe my stomach's talking to you now,
since I just had dinner
with one of the more notorious

figures I gather I will ever
encounter. He called me

Dear. I had, two days before,
dreamed he called me Darling.

See how I settle for less.

Storylines

The way things are going, children
will have to upgrade to more amusing.
No one could say that when
the highway snapped in two,
he saved her, then wandered off
and later did not remember. In hell,
on an airplane, in a theater, on a tightrope
made of light—no one said there was
no plot, but everything fell where
it belonged and roused conflicting
ecstasies. There is no paper, no pages
to burn. He saved her but did not
see her. He and his friend tried
to resurrect a man they both had
spoken with, but since they could not
agree, the third person doesn't exist.
How is anyone kissing anyone
possible. Events have to poke
through almost every story; it's how
they work, otherwise more people will
feel disappointed. A parking lot
where couples go to argue, a neighbor
looking cautiously down—to be caught
watching is to enter the argument,
which changes its character.
Another relationship to narrative,
almost legible. Next, no children
at the party, but everyone wants
pictures of the dog. The store
closing, the train stopping, the man
the others know and then evade.
What lay over the hill was unavailable

before they stepped into their voices.
Not singing, no song to describe.
Even the boys check their hands when
someone says GIRL HOLDING A SNAKE,
to make sure they aren't the girl.

Clouds Mistaken for Nearby Clouds

You could resist a melody
but who will be killed
if one just appears,
as a moon in daylight might.
If I believed in god
I'd thank it for making
irony: tiny neon frogs
and baroque jellyfish
so beautiful they can
go ahead and kill you
without even having
to feel like it.
Hush, everyone
screaming down there,
we can't hear the new
album everyone loves,
you have to be serious
all the time or else
everyone dies. Well,

Two More

Probability: If I had a llama
I wouldn't mind if he chewed

on my sleeve a little. If you have a llama
you should have two or three, otherwise

they get lonely even in your house. Liability:
When you look at my face you can see

that my heart gyrates like a pollywog.
Probability, gyrating   "   "   "   .

Probability: Gender!
Liability: When a celebrity

gets cancer, that kind of cancer
gets famous but insists it doesn't want to

be treated any differently. Probability:
The distance does the winking,

not the boat vanishing in it,
not the sun ramming through it.

This Land Is Mylar

balloons collapsing

onto sites of un-

speakable sadness,

it's an orchestra
whose conductor

wags a corn dog   at the horns.

This land of ours
eats up marches
and techno
and heartstrings
and spit-shined schadenfreude.

If you get hurt at the circus

you have to join—

no better way to see

this land,

which a big bland hand shook out

like a sheet   and everywhere

shit went flying,

some of which was us.

A Small Gesture of Gratitude

I have to tell you something. There is an *actor* in the world
called Joaquin Phoenix, and he's been *acting* pretty strangely
lately (messy beard, monosyllables, not promoting random

blockbuster, etc.). Two robots who embody barely one
percent of everything worth hating about the media were
on a 24-hour news channel "analyzing" his "controversial"

interview with David Letterman, a talk-show host.
These polished zombies were speculating about "this whole
controversy" under unkind studio lights, quizzing each

other about whether this *actor* is *acting* or actually crazy
or on "drugs"—desperately dry-humping the finer points
of one of the least crucial issues of our moment—

and whether the talk-show host, who all but patented
mainstream deadpan irony, was in fact pissed off
at this *actor* for appearing on his eponymous talk show

and creating a "controversy" that the human lampreys
who dole out the news with coffee spoons could fasten
themselves to, thus escalating ratings, ad sales, etc.

I have to tell you that I was in a public place, scribbling
about this completely irrelevant but also kind of excellent
Warholian non-interview, and at the very moment my pen

was poking into said cloud of pop-culture effluvium,
I overheard two women behind me, talking about the self-
same non-controversy—let's just call it a nontroversy:

I think it's an act I think he's crazy He's on drugs I don't think
so You don't? But I can't turn around because I'm afraid
that if I see their faces—let alone make eye contact,

acknowledging in even the smallest way that I am complicit
in the nontroversy—a huge blood-crusted mortar and pestle
will descend from the ceiling and grind my head into a paste.

TV news is killing us and the people who own it are killing us
and the criminals at whose behest they concoct more nontroversies
are killing us and the tons of hairspray and makeup they smear

on the toxic marionettes who mouth nontroversies are killing us,
as is our ignorance of the reality of everyone killing everyone.
If it's true to say the incubus fills us for the succubi to suck us dry,

why shouldn't I? Pointing into bottomless, topless, sideless
madness is what scads of poets do and have been doing all along:
we take facts and/or feelings, herd them like butterflies

into killing jars, then run pins through them for the aesthetic
and/or ethical scrutiny of a tiny audience made mostly of other
butterfly-killers. I have to tell you something else:

I have "invented" and am promoting a neologism
for the perineum: the boyband—as in,
"I'm walking funny 'cause I just had my boyband waxed"—

injecting something useless into the lexicon, if you will;
messing on a micro level with the zeitgeist, if you won't.
I've been running this new term—the boyband—

by a number of people recently, thus exposing
and/or confirming myself as the frivolous, vulgar idiot
I frequently am or *act* like; but that's the kind of behavior

everyone has come to expect from Americans anyway,
so I am in this sense as American as anyone else.
This poem is turning into a shuddering black hole

of broken rules, much like the Cheney/Bush regime,
albeit silly rules I tend to bray at my students about not
breaking: referring to the poem itself and (worse) to myself

writing it, invoking Penelope and Eliot and celebrities,
hawking awkward similes, referring to "teaching poetry,"
overusing quotes and/or italics, pay no attention to tenses,

not caring whether I've inadvertently stolen
a phrase or an image, deploying the word "reality," etc.
Maybe certain poets should have breathalyzers

connected to their computers or typewriters or hands
so they can't do what I'm doing right now to this poem.
Next week, if I accidentally meet President Obama

because someone I adore performs an amazing feat or merely
something "controversial," gets invited to the White House,
needs a plus-one, figures I'm good for a laugh, brings

me along, and I get 15 seconds of face time with
our new commander in chief, I'll just fuck it up: forget
to mention Prop 8 or Darfur or health care or education,

instead squawk some idiocy about how I've decided
we should all call the taint the boyband or hey,
what about that Joaquin Phoenix, so crazy! Maybe not

as scandalous as Grace Slick, a singer, who came *this* close
to dosing Richard Nixon, another president, with LSD, a drug;
but either way, whether Obama cracks up laughing,

high-fives me and says, *Yeah, but what about the girlgroup?*
or has the secret service 86 me, or barely blinks and moves on
to the next guest, some perfect mound of reptilian excrement

like Rush Limbaugh will catch wind of this non-event and funnel
it into one of his flatulent Hindenburgs of "controversy,"
so folks can be distracted by "that whole boyband thing,"

or christen it Taintgate—once a thing has a -gate, you can stop
calling the thing "that whole _____thing"—and I'll take
only this notoriety to my early grave. Nonetheless, I'll be known

for *something*—like Penelope, who loomed, or Orpheus, who lyred.
By the way, thanks for nothing E. Spitzer, R. Burris, T. Daschle,
R. Blagor;asld,gkjp—at least S. Palin isn't, at the time of this

concocting, melting our collective American face off
with her down-home hubris, end-times agendas and meth-
cooking, wolf-killing kin. Has anyone else come up

with the phrase *lipstick on a Dick* yet? Probably—I call
it The Anxiety of Coincidence (see above for annoying
tics). So much to do, so many rules to redo. But now,

my beloved friend who takes me to the White House,
unwitting kindling for the media blaze, I tell you
this: I'm sorry. Also, you're welcome. And to those

witnesses who prefer to be protected from poems
and butterflies, I tell you that I'm sorry some insidious force
led you here, but that you, maybe most of all, are welcome.

About the Author

Mark Bibbins is the author of two previous collections of poems, *The Dance of No Hard Feelings* and the Lambda Award-winning *Sky Lounge*. He teaches in the graduate writing programs of The New School, where he cofounded *LIT* magazine, and Columbia University. He edits the poetry section of *The Awl*.

Lannan Literary Selections

For two decades Lannan Foundation has supported the publication and distribution of exceptional literary works. Copper Canyon Press gratefully acknowledges their support.

LANNAN LITERARY SELECTIONS 2014

Mark Bibbins, *They Don't Kill You Because They're Hungry, They Kill You Because They're Full*

Malachi Black, *Storm Toward Morning*

Marianne Boruch, *Cadaver, Speak*

Jericho Brown, *The New Testament*

Olena Kalytiak Davis, *The Poem She Didn't Write and Other Poems*

RECENT LANNAN LITERARY SELECTIONS FROM COPPER CANYON PRESS

James Arthur, *Charms Against Lightning*

Natalie Diaz, *When My Brother Was an Aztec*

Matthew Dickman and Michael Dickman, *50 American Plays*

Michael Dickman, *Flies*

Kerry James Evans, *Bangalore*

Tung-Hui Hu, *Greenhouses, Lighthouses*

Laura Kasischke, *Space, in Chains*

Deborah Landau, *The Last Usable Hour*

Sarah Lindsay, *Debt to the Bone-Eating Snotflower*

Michael McGriff, *Home Burial*

Valzhyna Mort, *Collected Body*

Lisa Olstein, *Little Stranger*

Roger Reeves, *King Me*

Ed Skoog, *Rough Day*

John Taggart, *Is Music: Selected Poems*

Jean Valentine, *Break the Glass*

Dean Young, *Fall Higher*

For a complete list of Lannan Literary Selections from Copper Canyon Press, please visit Partners on our website: www.coppercanyonpress.org

Poetry is vital to language and living. Since 1972, Copper Canyon Press has published extraordinary poetry from around the world to engage the imaginations and intellects of readers, writers, booksellers, librarians, teachers, students, and donors.

WE ARE GRATEFUL FOR THE MAJOR SUPPORT PROVIDED BY:

THE PAUL G. ALLEN
FAMILY FOUNDATION

THE MAURER FAMILY
FOUNDATION

NATIONAL
ENDOWMENT
FOR THE ARTS

WASHINGTON STATE
ARTS COMMISSION

Anonymous
John Branch
Diana and Jay Broze
Beroz Ferrell & The Point, llc
Janet and Les Cox
Mimi Gardner Gates
Gull Industries, Inc.
on behalf of William and Ruth True
Mark Hamilton and Suzie Rapp
Carolyn and Robert Hedin
Steven Myron Holl
Lakeside Industries, Inc.
on behalf of Jeanne Marie Lee
Maureen Lee and Mark Busto
Brice Marden
H. Stewart Parker
Penny and Jerry Peabody
John Phillips and Anne O'Donnell
Joseph C. Roberts
Cynthia Lovelace Sears and Frank Buxton
The Seattle Foundation
Dan Waggoner
Charles and Barbara Wright
The dedicated interns and faithful
volunteers of Copper Canyon Press

To learn more about underwriting Copper Canyon Press titles,
please call 360-385-4925 ext. 103